power mood

MINDSET WORKBOOK

*Achieve Your Career Goals
with Intention and Confidence*

Sam DeMase

ROCK POINT

For my grandma Jo, who would be so proud to read this, and grandma Margie, who is always on my side.

Contents

INTRODUCTION

How to Use This Workbook

Welcome to the *Power Mood Mindset Workbook*! Hopefully, you've read my companion book, *Power Mood*, but if not, no worries! This workbook will be covering all the same concepts, but via a more hands-on approach. Your Power Mood originates in those moments that clarify your purpose. It's an individual expression that changes with you over time. As you figure out what motivates you, what you care about, and what you need to be your best self, your Power Mood grows.

When you discover your superpowers (the things you do better than anyone else), use them to your advantage, and support and uplift others, your Power Mood also grows. Getting to know yourself and celebrating all of your beautifully unique qualities is part of the journey to finding your Power Mood.

HOW TO USE THIS WORKBOOK

I designed this workbook not only to help you hack the corporate system and learn how to advocate for yourself in the workplace, but also to give you a place to discover new things about yourself. It will help you set new goals and celebrate your wins. There are seven different activities, all of which require your participation:

1. **Thought Starters:** Prompts that pique your curiosity and help you examine a specific topic more thoroughly.

2. **Checklists:** Lists from which you choose the items that apply to you and/or your work situation.

3. **Quizzes:** Multiple-choice questions about specific topics. Listen to your gut as you make your selections, and then reflect on your results.

4. **Templates:** Structured charts and graphs you can fill in with your own information to prepare for specific actions.

5. **Power Mood Boards:** Space to doodle, freewrite, jot down notes, and reflect on what you've learned in each section.

6. **Role-Plays:** Practicing specific situations out loud, either on your own or with a partner. These will help you build confidence and retain important information.

7. **Power Pauses:** Intentional breaks at the end of each section to focus on and celebrate your wins.

Before most of the activities, you'll find a Power Memo that contains more information about each topic. However, to get the full benefit of each exercise, it's important that you do more than simply follow the instructions; be mindful of your thoughts as you go through them because that's how you might strike gold! For example, you might be checking items off a list or filling out a template when a real gem hits you hard and changes the game.

When that happens, be sure to share what you discovered with a friend. We need this workplace self-advocacy knowledge to spread far and wide because we are stronger as a collective.

So, grab your favorite pen and get ready to write all over this thing. Let this workbook be your confidence-boosting roadmap to finding your path, your voice, and your power.

CONFIDENCE CHECK-IN

1. How would you rate your overall confidence in your current ability to build a compelling resume?

   ○ Not at all confident.
   ○ Low confidence.
   ○ Somewhat confident.
   ○ Confident.
   ○ Extremely confident.

2. How would you rate your overall confidence in your interviewing skills?

   ○ Not at all confident.
   ○ Low confidence.
   ○ Somewhat confident.
   ○ Confident.
   ○ Extremely confident.

3. How would you rate your overall confidence in your negotiation skills?

   ○ Not at all confident.
   ○ Low confidence.
   ○ Somewhat confident.
   ○ Confident.
   ○ Extremely confident.

4. How would you rate your overall confidence in your workplace communication skills?

   ○ Not at all confident.
   ○ Low confidence.
   ○ Somewhat confident.
   ○ Confident.
   ○ Extremely confident.

5. How would you rate your overall confidence in boundary-setting?
   ○ Not at all confident.
   ○ Low confidence.
   ○ Somewhat confident.
   ○ Confident.
   ○ Extremely confident.

6. How would you rate your overall confidence in your self-advocacy skills?
   ○ Not at all confident.
   ○ Low confidence.
   ○ Somewhat confident.
   ○ Confident.
   ○ Extremely confident.

7. Which skills are you most hoping to improve by completing this workbook? Check all that apply:
   ○ Building a compelling resume.
   ○ Interview skills.
   ○ Negotiation skills.
   ○ Workplace communication.
   ○ Setting boundaries.
   ○ Advocating for myself.

CALCULATE YOUR RESULTS

Now, take a look at how you rated yourself. Do you notice any patterns? Are there certain areas in which you struggle more than others? Engaging thoughtfully in this way with the activities in this workbook will help you build your confidence in those areas. It will also supply you with the necessary tools to successfully navigate these situations in the future.

From resume building and interviewing, to negotiating and setting healthy workplace boundaries, you'll learn how to integrate your unique superpowers into every aspect of your career, from the job search to asking for a promotion.

After you finish this workbook, take the Confidence Check-In Quiz again—you'll be astounded at how your answers have changed.

To conjure
your Power Mood,
you have to get
to know yourself
with intention.

PART I: CONJURING

Conjuring is your career-confidence foundation, and it all begins with getting to know your superpowers. You'll then use these as a base on which to build a compelling, achievements-focused resume. Using my proprietary frameworks, you will also learn how to interview with newfound confidence. Finally, practice will help you get comfortable with using collaborative language to negotiate your salary like a pro!

In this section, you'll identify your superpowers, as well as what you need to be your best self at work. You'll also define your core values so you can more easily find your ideal work environment.

The common theme that runs through this entire section is that preparation breeds confidence. The activities will ensure that you're prepared for anything, whether it's an interview, negotiation, or knowing if an environment will work for you.

Each element builds on the one before it, so by the time we get to the negotiation phase, you'll be fully prepared to advocate for what you're worth and command your value!

CHAPTER 1

The Power Mood Mindset

Get ready to inhabit your Power Mood! The first ingredient in this recipe is pinpointing what makes you, *you*. To do this, you have to think deeply about your passions and skill sets because this is where your Power Mood begins. Finding confidence starts with naming what makes you unique and celebrating it.

The activities in this chapter require you to dig deep into the essence of who you are so you can discover the things you do better than anyone else.

It's important to define and celebrate these unique facets of you, as that is where your superpowers come from, and they form the foundation of your ultimate career confidence.

WHAT MAKES YOU, *YOU*?

INTENTION: Get to know your strengths so you can inhabit your Power Mood.

Honing in on the traits and skills that make you awesome is key to discovering your Power Mood. Check all of the words and phrases below that describe you the most accurately, then add a few of your own in the blank spaces:

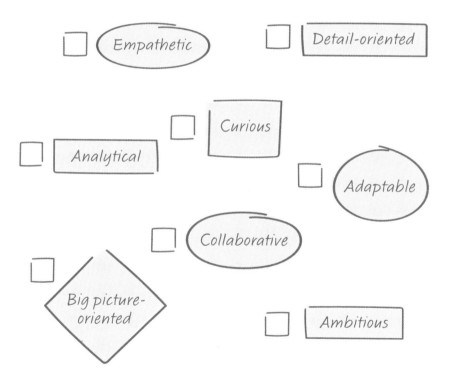

- ☐ Empathetic
- ☐ Detail-oriented
- ☐ Curious
- ☐ Analytical
- ☐ Adaptable
- ☐ Collaborative
- ☐ Big picture-oriented
- ☐ Ambitious

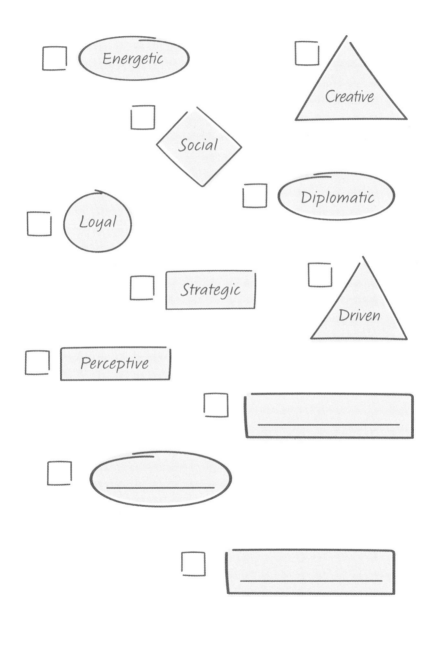

Energetic

Creative

Social

Diplomatic

Loyal

Strategic

Driven

Perceptive

ASK YOUR BEST FRIEND TO WRITE YOUR BIO

INTENTION: Allow someone who knows you well to write about you and your talents and abilities, and then you do the same for them.

Just about everyone finds it easy to hype up the positive traits of others, but not their own. This is why it can be helpful for your best friend to write a four- or five-sentence bio about you, and then you do the same for them. Read what you wrote about each other; did either of you highlight any traits or skills about the other that surprised you?

EMBRACE YOUR QUIRKINESS

INTENTION: Acknowledge, embrace, and share your unique interests, skills, and talents.

Bringing your whole self to work includes the more unusual aspects of your personality, as well. These are things you may tend to hide. For example, perhaps you collect vintage tea cozies or play a mean game of tennis. When you share your interests at work, it makes it easier to find those with whom you have common ground.

List a few things below that you usually don't share with your coworkers, but plan to do so at your next job:

CHAPTER 2

Finding Your Career Path

The next step to inhabiting your Power Mood and discovering your confidence is to define your "why." This is what motivates you and will help you discover and articulate your superpowers. Your superpowers are the things you do better than anyone else. They're what you're known for, and when they're articulated powerfully, they can land you that awesome high-paying job you want and deserve.

Once you've defined your superpowers, you will use this information to establish the parameters for the kind of work environment in which you can thrive. It's important to be intentional about this process; too often, I see folks jump into careers that are not well-suited to their superpowers or core values.

When you take the time to explore yourself, and what you want and need, you set yourself up for a future that is more deeply aligned with who you are. The goal is to find a career that suits your lifestyle, not a lifestyle that suits your career.

DEFINING YOUR TOP FIVE CORE VALUES

INTENTION: Identify your core values so you know what type of work environment you require to grow and thrive.

Your core values are your "non-negotiables"—the things you require to do your best work. Your ideal career path and workplace environment should share most (if not all) of these.

What are eight to ten things you value most in life (such as independence, family, creativity, humor, community, growth, learning, inclusiveness, money, and so on)?

1 ....
2 ....
3 ....
4 ....
5 ....
6 ....
7 ....
8 ....
9 ....
10 ....

Now, narrow that list down to your top five:

1 ....
2 ....
3 ....
4 ....
5 ....

Finally, rank those top five in order of importance:

1 ....
2 ....
3 ....
4 ....
5 ....

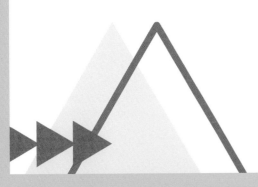

WHAT IS A SUPERPOWER?

Your most potent superpowers are where your passions and skill sets converge. For example, if you have a passion for teamwork and a skill set in public speaking, one of your superpowers might just be people leadership.

Some other examples of superpowers include:

- Ability to tell compelling stories.
- Capable of seeing the big picture.
- Easily absorbing complex information.
- Being a creative force.
- Quickly spotting flaws and knowing how to fix them.
- Creating structure out of ambiguity.
- Being a skilled researcher.
- The ability to pitch and sell anything.
- Being an excellent public speaker.
- Bringing out the best in others.

WHAT ARE YOUR PASSIONS AND SKILLS?

INTENTION: Recognizing and owning the things you do better than anyone else.

Again, your superpowers are those things you do better than anyone else; the things you are known for. Ideally, they are also things that you enjoy doing, so we'll start there.

List four or five things you enjoy doing more than anything else (these are your passions):

1 ....

2 ....

3 ....

4 ....

5 ....

Now, what are some things you do better than anyone else? These are your skill sets. If you have any trouble coming up with these, ask your friends and family what they think you are best at:

1 ....

2 ....

3 ....

4 ....

5 ....

DEFINING YOUR SUPERPOWERS

INTENTION: Define your superpowers so you can highlight them during your job search.

Before you can emphasize your value on your resume or during negotiations, you must first define your superpowers, and writing them down is the first step. Follow the example in the chart below; in the results column, include metrics, such as timelines, dollar amounts, percentages, and so on.

SUPERPOWER	EXAMPLE OF SUPERPOWER IN ACTION	RESULTS ACHIEVED AFTER DEPLOYING SUPERPOWER
Expert problem-solver and quick thinker.	*Resolved escalated cases for clients and delivered exceptional customer service.*	*Retained a high-profile client who was at risk of leaving and increased their total contract spend by 15 percent.*

TALKING ABOUT YOUR SUPERPOWERS

INTENTION: Being completely comfortable articulating your superpowers.

The ability to speak seamlessly and confidently about your superpowers is a superpower itself! It's also a very necessary one when it comes to job interviews and negotiating salary.

To get more comfortable with talking about your awesomeness, write down each of your superpowers followed by an example of it in action with metrics. Then, ask a friend or a family member to ask why they should hire you so you can practice answering:

PINPOINT YOUR IDEAL WORK ENVIRONMENT

INTENTION: Know the type of environment you need to deliver your best work.

Your work environment has a big impact on you both emotionally and mentally. It also affects your productivity. This is why, before you interview for a job, it's important to know what type of work environment will suit you best.

Think about what you need to feel at ease and deliver your best work. Then, check off the environmental characteristics from the following list that would enable you to do that and add a few of your own:

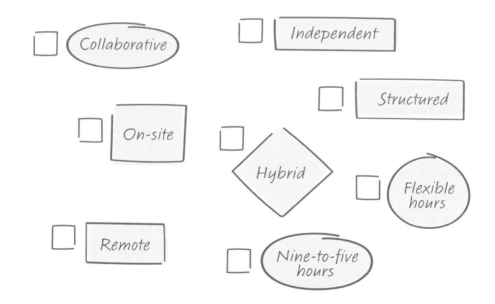

☐ Collaborative

☐ Independent

☐ Structured

☐ On-site

☐ Hybrid

☐ Flexible hours

☐ Remote

☐ Nine-to-five hours

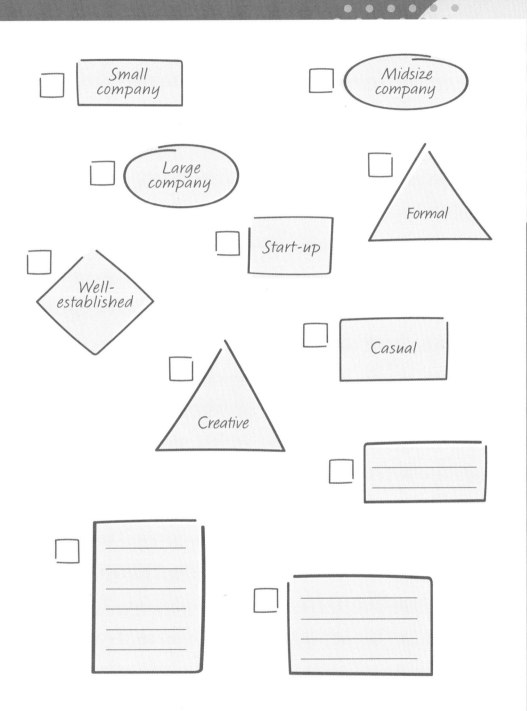

Small
company

Midsize
company

Large
company

Formal

Start-up

Well-
established

Casual

Creative

CHAPTER 3

The Resume Remodel

Transforming your resume from a regurgitation of your past job descriptions into a powerful story about your achievements is a key ingredient in your confidence recipe. It will also be the foundation of your job search—and you want that foundation to be rock solid.

A resume is the platform on which you should showcase your superpowers and achievements—and most people undersell themselves on it. It should be compelling, while also telling your story and celebrating what makes you powerful.

This is also where you take credit for your accomplishments. It is not the time to share credit with your colleagues—your resume should be all about *you* and *your* skills and achievements. Its goal is singular: to get you job interviews! It should also be something you're proud of and feel excited to send out, and if that's not where it is now, let the resume remodel begin!

TRANSFORM PASSIVE VERBS INTO DYNAMIC VERBS

INTENTION: Take credit for your work and tell your story effectively.

Does your resume include words like coordinated, facilitated, performed, assisted, and/or helped? A few of these sprinkled in is perfectly fine if it's accurate. However, if you have a lot of those (or if your resume is exclusively made up of passive verbs), we need to transform those into *dynamic* verbs.

Dynamic verbs are more action-oriented, like "spearheaded," "led," and "strategized." For example, instead of saying "Performed administrative duties," you could say, "Managed all administrative tasks, including filing, auditing, and scheduling." You've worked hard and had an impact at all of your jobs, so don't undersell yourself.

On the following list, check off all the dynamic verbs that resonate the most with your past or current job functions (add any that aren't listed, as well), and add them all to your resume where applicable:

☐ Created

☐ Directed

☐ Launched

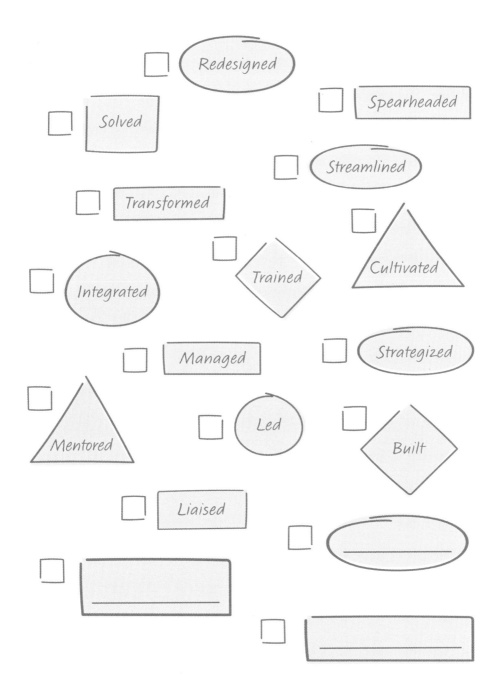

☐ Redesigned

☐ Solved

☐ Spearheaded

☐ Streamlined

☐ Transformed

☐ Cultivated

☐ Integrated

☐ Trained

☐ Managed

☐ Strategized

☐ Mentored

☐ Led

☐ Built

☐ Liaised

☐

☐

☐

PASSIVE VS. DYNAMIC VERBS

INTENTION: Communicate ownership and action to hiring managers on your resume.

When you use language on your resume that conveys ownership, it speaks volumes to recruiters and hiring managers. For example, instead of "Provided exceptional customer service," you might say "Delivered industry-leading customer service."

In the chart below, write the first word of each bullet point in the work experience section of your resume in the first column. Review the verb checklist on the previous page; are there any stronger, more active verbs you could use instead? If so, write the dynamic verb in the second column.

PASSIVE VERB	DYNAMIC VERB

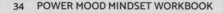

THE RESUME GLOW-UP

INTENTION: Turn your work experience into measurable achievements.

Another feature that will make your resume really stand out is turning your work experience into measurable achievements. Say one of your job duties was "filing paperwork." When you turn that into a measurable achievement, it might say something like, "Maintained 100 percent compliance for all audits from 2019–2020."

In the chart below, write your new dynamic bullet points from the previous exercise in the first column. In the second column, include metrics (timelines, percentages, and so on).

DYNAMIC VERSION OF WORK EXPERIENCE	METRICS

SASHA TAYLOR (SHE/HER)
Digital Marketing Analyst

ABOUT ME

Digital Marketing Analyst with five years' experience in the retail space. I craft innovative campaigns, build strategic partnerships, and deliver exceptional results for clients.

ACHIEVEMENTS

- Launched SEO campaign that generated 10,000 unique visitors and 200 customers monthly.
- Developed customer-focused email campaign that improved monthly retention rate by 20 percent.

SKILLS

- Salesforce
- Google Analytics
- SEO
- Spanish language

CONTACT

sashataylor@samplemail.com
555-802-3976
linkedin.com/in/sashab

EXPERIENCE

Digital Marketing Analyst
Tildwell Fashions, New York, NY
(2017–Present)

- Manage SEO campaigns with budget of $50K.
- Oversee insight development workshop for four activation teams weekly to deliver actionable reporting to client.
- Create reporting tools to allow for real-time adjustment of paid ad strategy, leading to $200K in incremental revenue.

Digital Marketing Coordinator
Carter & Scone, New York, NY
(2015–2017)

- Owned planning for $10 million social media budget, driving $5 million in revenue in 2017.
- Led billing for $20 million client, ensuring all publishing partners were paid on time.
- Increased ROI 10 percent by shifting to more relevant publishers against target audience groups.

EDUCATION

Smith College (2010–2014)
BA, Psychology

THE SEVEN ESSENTIAL RESUME SECTIONS

> **INTENTION:** Update your resume so it includes the essential information recruiters and hiring managers are looking for.

It's time to make sure your resume has all the essential information, and that it is arranged in the correct order. Using the sample resume on the previous page as a guide, sketch out each section of your resume below. Remember to use clear and compelling language, and take credit for your accomplishments.

Headline (current or most recent job title and industry):

About Me (a few sentences about your superpowers and experience):

Achievements (a few of your proudest accomplishments):

Work Experience (achievements, quantified with metrics):

....

....

....

....

Contact (email, phone number, and LinkedIn profile):

....

....

Certifications and Skills (software, coursework, languages, and so on):

....

....

....

Education (school(s), degree(s), and so on):

....

....

....

HOW TO WRITE AN IMPACTFUL COVER LETTER

Your cover letter is the first opportunity you have to communicate your skills concisely, clearly, and powerfully, in addition to why they make you right for that particular role.

It's important that you resist the temptation to just rehash your resume in your cover letter. Always personalize it to the specific position to which you're applying and keep it short (around three paragraphs).

I have a formula that will help you do all of the above, and I call it the ESP method:

- **ELABORATE:** Explain why you are excited about the role and quote the job description.

- **SPECIFY:** Explain why you are a great fit and cite at least two specific examples (with metrics) of related work experience.

- **PARALLEL:** Link your values to those of the company (you can usually find this info in the Mission or Values section of the company's website). Describe what you are passionate about and how this aligns with the company.

Here's a sample cover letter that uses the ESP method:

Hello Natalie,

I'm thrilled to apply for the VP of Training role at [company] because my ten years of experience leading cross-functional training teams aligns perfectly with this opportunity.

I am incredibly passionate about equipping people with user-friendly learning tools and building enthusiastic teams. This role gets me pumped, as it involves precisely what I love to do. (**Elaborate**)

I know you're seeking someone who is a builder, and that's what I do best. In my current role, I created six new full-time training roles and increased training completion rates by 75 percent. (**Specify**)

The mission and values of [company] also completely align with my own. As a sustainable shopper, your brand proposition is inspiring (I swear by your reusable bags). (**Parallel**)

I would love to bring my experience and passion for training to [company]. Thank you, and I look forward to continuing the conversation.

Best,

[Your name]

USE **ESP** TO WRITE YOUR NEXT COVER LETTER

INTENTION: Link your skills and experience to the job for which you are applying.

Now it's your turn! Use the cover letter on the previous page to write your own for the next position to which you want to apply. Fill in the details below utilizing the ESP formula:

Hello, _____
[Hiring manager's name]

I'm thrilled to apply for the _____ role
[Position]

at _____. My _____ experience in
[Company]   [Number of months/years]

_____ aligns perfectly with this opportunity.
[Position and/or industry]

I'm incredibly passionate about _____. (**Elaborate**)
[Aspect(s) of role from job description]

I know you're seeking someone who is a _____,
[Aspect of role that links to your job experience]

and that's what I do best. In my _____ role as _____,
[Current/previous]   [Job title]

I _____ and _____. (**Specify**)
[Past experience with metrics]   [Past experience with metrics]

The mission and values of _____ also align so well
[Company]

with my own. Your _____ is inspiring because
[Company mission or value]

_____. (**Parallel**)
[Link to a value or passion of your own]

I would love to bring my experience in _____,
[Aspect of role that links to your job experience]

to _____.
[Company]

Thank you, and I look forward to continuing the conversation.

Best,

_____
[Your name]

CHAPTER 4

Crushing the Interview

Job interviews can be intimidating, especially if you're new at them or haven't had one in a while. In this chapter, we'll break the process down into manageable activities, and you'll soon find that they aren't as scary as you once thought.

Luckily, interviews are often predictable, which means you can prepare in advance and set yourself up for a win.

There are three phases to successful interviewing: prep, the interview conversation, and the follow-up. The activities in this chapter will transform the way you approach this process and turn interviews into job offers.

Also, always keep in mind that an interview is a *conversation*, not an *interrogation*. This is an important Power Mood mindset to have both before and during your interview because it's easy to get overwhelmed and forget that *you* are also interviewing *them*.

PREPARATION IS KEY

Pre-interview nerves stem from the fear of the unknown. What will they ask you? What if you don't know the answer? What do they care about, anyway? By doing some intentional research beforehand, you will already be ten steps ahead as soon as you walk in the door.

If you simply check out the following areas ahead of time and jot down some notes, you'll be ready for just about anything they throw at you:

- **Research the people:** This might allow you to uncover something you have in common with them, so you can weave it into the interview conversation. For example, maybe you went to the same school, come from the same area, or have mutual friends or former colleagues.

- **Review the company's mission and values:** Not only is this important for the interview, but it will also let you know whether your core values align with theirs. Note anything that resonates with you, so you can be prepared to discuss it when they ask what appealed to you about the company.

- **Note any company news:** Perhaps they've launched a new product line or just went public on the stock exchange. If so, you'll want to be aware if they bring it up, or you can weave it into the conversation and impress them with your thorough research.

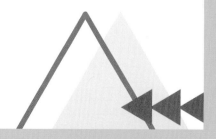

INTERVIEW PREP

> **INTENTION:** Find out as much as you can about the company ahead of time, so you can make the best impression possible.

Visit the company's website, and then answer the following prompts prior to your interview.

Look up the person you'll be meeting with on the company directory or LinkedIn. Do you have anything common? If so, list them below:

....

....

....

Visit the Mission and/or Values section on the company's website and list any specific areas where your values and theirs align:

....

....

....

Visit the company's blog or search Google for any current news. List any new or upcoming products, launches, initiatives, and so on you want to be prepared to talk about:

....

....

....

THE **WAT** INTERVIEW METHOD

One of the most dreaded points in any job interview is when the interviewer says, "Tell me about yourself." Many candidates simply rehash their entire resume, while others talk about their personal life and hobbies. While you can certainly sprinkle in the latter, neither of these is what the interviewer really wants to know.

What they want to know is, quite simply, why they should hire you. If you outline your case clearly, they will immediately be able to envision you in that role, and my WAT method enables you to do just that. So, what exactly is WAT? I'm so glad you asked!

- **W**hat you do: Your resume headline.
- **A**chievements: The things you've accomplished that relate to the role.
- **T**ie-in: Why you are excited about the role, and how it will utilize at least one of your superpowers.

Here's an example of the WAT method in action:

Interviewer: *Tell me about yourself.*

Interviewee: *I'm a training and development leader with over six years of experience in the hospitality space (**W**). In my most recent role, I launched a brand-new Learning Management System, which increased employee training completion rates by 50 percent (**A**). I know you're looking for someone who is a results-driven builder with experience launching a new LMS, which is exactly what I'm passionate about, so I'm really excited to discuss this role (**T**).*

PREP YOUR **WAT**-METHOD ANSWER

INTENTION: Prepare the right answer for the old "tell me about yourself" interview question.

Answer the following prompts to effectively plan your WAT-method response when an interviewer says, "Tell me about yourself.":

What is the headline on your resume (**W**)?

....

....

List several past achievements that relate to the role for which you're being interviewed (**A**):

....

....

Why are you excited about this role? Provide a tie-in with your previous experience that also highlights a superpower (**T**):

....

....

....

....

Now, put it all together in one cohesive response:

....

....

....

....

ANSWERING COMMON BEHAVIORAL QUESTIONS WITH THE **CARE** METHOD

At most job interviews, you'll likely be asked at least a few behavioral questions, which include things like:

- What are your greatest strengths?
- What are some of your weaknesses or areas that need improvement?
- Tell me about a time that you made a mistake at work.
- Have you ever disagreed with your leader or a colleague? How did you handle it?
- Can you share an example of a time when you pulled together as a team under challenging circumstances?
- Describe a situation in which you delivered a big win for a client or internal stakeholder.
- Have you ever improved an existing process or created a new one? Tell me about that.

The CARE method is a foolproof way of answering behavioral interview questions.

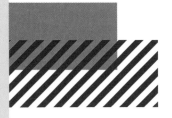

CARE stands for:

- **C**ontext: The situation at hand at a high level.
- **A**ction: The action you took to solve the problem.
- **R**esult: What happened based on the action you took.
- **E**volution: How managing this situation helped you improve or learn new skills.

Here is an example of a stellar response to, "Tell me about a time you made a mistake at work.":

"At my last job I was in charge of a project that involved multiple stakeholders. (**Context**) I accidentally sent an important email to the wrong person. As a result, there was a brief delay in the project timeline. I owned up to it, corrected my mistake (**Action**), and we quickly got back on track. (**Result**)

I tend to be a big-picture thinker, so this taught me a lot about the importance of honing in on the fine details. At the time, I was hard on myself, but now I realize that this made me a much more detail-oriented project manager." (**Evolution**)

THE **CARE** METHOD IN ACTION

INTENTION: Having strong answers prepared for the most common behavioral interview questions.

To eliminate interview jitters, it's important that you prep powerful responses to behavioral questions that highlight your superpowers. Choose three behavioral questions from the list on page 48, and then use the CARE method to fill in the template below with examples from your work experience.

Behavioral Question 1:

CONTEXT (THE CIRCUMSTANCES)	
ACTION (WHAT YOU DID)	
RESULT (THE OUTCOME OF YOUR ACTIONS)	
EVOLUTION (HOW YOU GREW AS A RESULT; HIGHLIGHT A SUPERPOWER)	

Behavioral Question 2: ....

CONTEXT (THE CIRCUMSTANCES)	
ACTION (WHAT YOU DID)	
RESULT (THE OUTCOME OF YOUR ACTIONS)	
EVOLUTION (HOW YOU GREW AS A RESULT; HIGHLIGHT A SUPERPOWER)	

Behavioral Question 3: ....

CONTEXT (THE CIRCUMSTANCES)	
ACTION (WHAT YOU DID)	
RESULT (THE OUTCOME OF YOUR ACTIONS)	
EVOLUTION (HOW YOU GREW AS A RESULT; HIGHLIGHT A SUPERPOWER)	

A MOCK JOB INTERVIEW

INTENTION: Practice your interview answers until you sound conversational and feel confident.

Whether you're new to job interviews or they just always make you nervous, practicing ahead of time makes a huge difference. Now that you've prepped your WAT responses and awesome CARE answers, it's time to try them out!

You can do this mock interview with a friend or by yourself. You can also video or audio record yourself to see how you appear and/or sound. Try to maintain slow, even pacing, and minimize the use of filler words (such as um, like, and so on). Also try to avoid upspeak (declarative statements that sound like questions).

Jot down your answers to all of the questions, and then have a friend ask them so you can practice out loud.

What are your biggest strengths?

What are your weaknesses/areas that need improvement?

Tell me about a time you made a mistake at work.

Describe a moment when you disagreed with a leader or colleague.

Describe a time you pulled together as a team under challenging circumstances.

Describe a time when you delivered a win for a client or stakeholder.

Describe how you improved a process or created a new one.

SPECIFIC QUESTIONS YOU SHOULD ASK DURING AN INTERVIEW

As you already learned, an interview is a conversation, not an interrogation. This means you should feel free to ask questions at any point—not just at the end. You might have role-specific questions, or questions about the company. Here are some examples of questions you might ask during a job interview:

- How is success defined and measured in this role?

- What's the onboarding and training process like for this role?

- What are the top goals for the person in this role to accomplish within the first three months?

- What are the biggest challenges the person in this role will face?

- What do you love most about working here?

- How have you grown since joining?

- What's next for the company?

- How does the company help its employees maintain a good work–life balance?

RED FLAGS

INTENTION: Learn to recognize the signs that a company isn't right for you.

Red flags at a job interview are usually pretty clear indications that it might be better to walk away. Review the following list of common red flags, check off any you noticed, and add any that aren't listed:

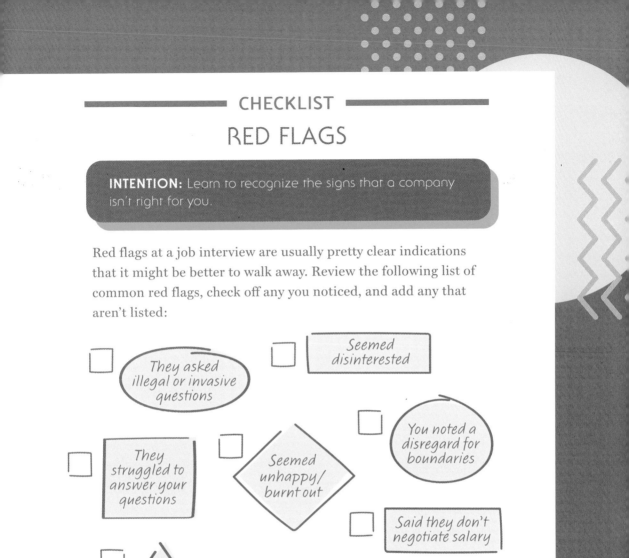

- ☐ They asked illegal or invasive questions
- ☐ Seemed disinterested
- ☐ They struggled to answer your questions
- ☐ Seemed unhappy/ burnt out
- ☐ You noted a disregard for boundaries
- ☐ Said they don't negotiate salary
- ☐ Spoke negatively about their employees
- ☐ No time for you to ask questions
- ☐ _____
- ☐ _____
- ☐ _____

GREEN FLAGS

INTENTION: Recognize the clear indicators that a job and company are right for you.

Of course, nothing (not even job interviews) are all gloom and doom—you should also be on the lookout for all the *good* things about a company! Just like you did with the red flags, review this list of *green* flags after each interview (make a copy or snap a pic of it to use after future interviews). Be sure to add any you noticed that aren't included:

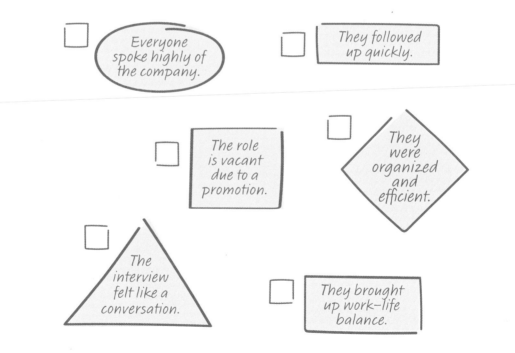

☐ Everyone spoke highly of the company.

☐ They followed up quickly.

☐ The role is vacant due to a promotion.

☐ They were organized and efficient.

☐ The interview felt like a conversation.

☐ They brought up work–life balance.

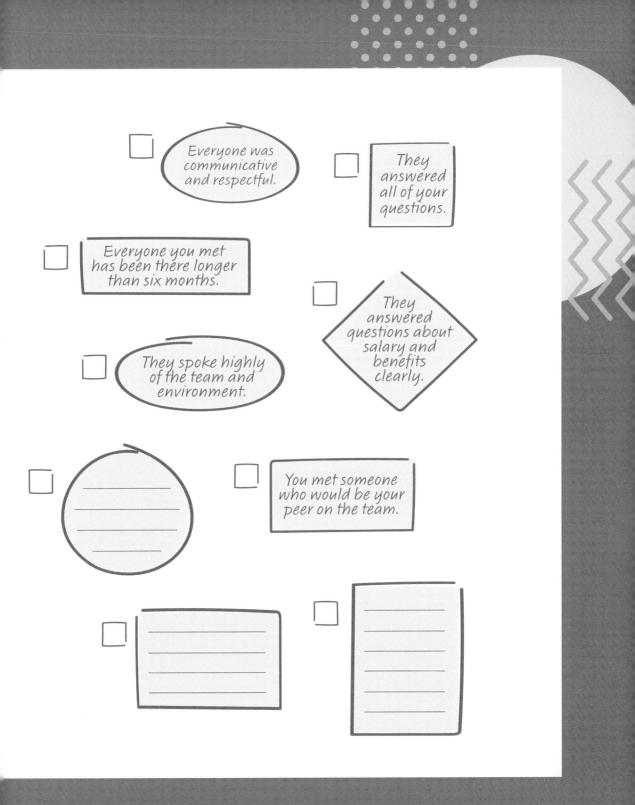

☐ Everyone was communicative and respectful.

☐ They answered all of your questions.

☐ Everyone you met has been there longer than six months.

☐ They answered questions about salary and benefits clearly.

☐ They spoke highly of the team and environment.

☐ _____

☐ You met someone who would be your peer on the team.

☐ _____

☐ _____

THE POST-INTERVIEW THANK-YOU

Sending a quick thank-you message after a job interview is essential because it further demonstrates that you are excited about the role. Send it within twenty-four hours after your interview. Later that same day is ideal because then, it will be one of the first emails they see when they check their inbox the next morning.

Thank-you emails should be brief, but memorable. Highlight something they said that excited you about the role, then mention one specific example from your job experience that directly prepares you to succeed in the role. Close by letting them know you're looking forward to continuing the conversation.

Here is an example of a strong thank-you email:

Hi Mariah,

Thanks so much for connecting with me today. Always a joy to chat with a fellow reality-show fan! I really enjoyed our conversation, hearing about [company], where the company is at currently, and the exciting challenges facing the Director of L&D role. You mentioned that building out the L&D team is an urgent priority, and team development is one of my passions and areas of expertise.

I have no doubt that my ten years of experience in L&D in the retail space, and zest for exceptional hospitality and stellar culture would be a great addition to your team.

Looking forward to continuing the conversation. Thanks again!

Best,
[Name]

WRITE A THANK-YOU EMAIL

INTENTION: Show your consideration for the interviewer's time and create another opportunity to express why you're perfect for the role.

After your next job interview, use the example on the previous page to fill in the blanks and construct your own thank-you email:

Hello, _____
      [Interviewer's name]

   Thank you so much for chatting with me today. It's always

a pleasure to meet a fellow _____ fan.
                            [Shared hobby/interest]

I really enjoyed our conversation about the _____
                                              [Position]

role at _____. The _____
        [Company]   [Challenges/priorities]

you mentioned for the _____ excited me because my
                       [Position]

experience as a _____ has made these my areas
                [Past role(s)]

of expertise.

   I have no doubt my _____ years of experience as a
                       [Number]

_____ in the _____
[Previous relevant position]   [Industry/job field]

and passion for _____ would make me
                 [Job Requirement]

an asset to your team. I look forward to continuing the conversation.

   Best,

_____
      [Your name]

THE POST-REJECTION EMAIL

Unfortunately, there will be times when it doesn't work out and you aren't selected for a job. As disappointing as this can be, keep in mind that it's part of the process.

If you found the interview process engaging and would like the company to keep you in mind for future opportunities, then by all means, respond to their rejection email.

Not only does this display professionalism, but perhaps the candidate they selected for the role won't work out. In that event, they might reach out to you to see if you are still available. Here's an example of what to write in your post-rejection email:

Hi Rosa,

Thank you again for the opportunity to interview. It has been a great experience. Getting to know the team confirmed my alignment with this company's core values. I look forward to following the growth you will no doubt be experiencing.

Please do keep me in mind for any future opportunities on the Content Marketing team.

Best,

[Your name]

WRITE A POST-REJECTION EMAIL

INTENTION: Keep the door open for future opportunities at a company.

If you liked a company you interviewed with and everything they stand for, responding to a rejection email could score you another opportunity later (or another shot at that same one if the person they hire doesn't work out).

Fill out the template below to compose a post-rejection email that could create an opportunity for you later:

Hello, _____,
                  [Interviewer's name]
   Thank you again for the opportunity to chat about the

_____ role at _____.
      [Position]   [Company]
   It was a pleasure meeting you and _____.
                                 [Others]
Doing so only further confirmed my alignment with

_____ core values. I look forward to following
     [Company's]
your growth and success.

   Please do keep me in mind for any future opportunities on

the _____ team.
           [Department]
   Best,

   _____
          [Your name]

CHAPTER 5

Nailing
the Negosh

Many people are intimidated by the idea of negotiating their salary, but where does this reticence come from?

At its heart, a salary negotiation is the act of advocating for what you feel you're worth in dollars and cents. If you don't feel confident about your worth, that's where the fear lies.

Now that you've worked to identify your superpowers, it's time to start believing in them!

Like interviewing, negotiation is a predictable process; it starts with research, then the collaborative negotiation conversation, and finally, the strategic evaluation of the offer on the table.

Negotiation is a *collaboration*, not a *confrontation*, and this is the essential Power Mood mindset you want to carry with you throughout the entire process.

SALARY NEGOTIATION FEARS AND BLOCKS

Whenever you start a new job, you are bringing your expertise, passion, experience, and unique superpowers to the table, and you should be compensated accordingly for all of that.

The more you negotiate, the more confident you will become. And don't be afraid of getting a "No"—that's actually where a negotiation begins. You should always negotiate your salary and here are just a few reasons why:

- **It's expected:** Companies anticipate that you will negotiate your salary.

- **To increase your self-worth:** Your confidence will improve every time you negotiate.

- **To make it easier for the next negotiation:** It will enhance your persuasion skills in both work and life.

- **To get what you deserve:** You are providing unique value and should be compensated accordingly.

- **To make it easier for those who follow:** Every time you negotiate, you raise the compensation bar for the next person.

- **To avoid having any regrets:** You won't be left wondering if you could have gotten more if you'd only asked.

CLARIFY YOUR "WHY"

INTENTION: Discover why negotiation is important to you.

Negotiating enables you to get the salary you deserve. It also builds your confidence and let's your new employer know that you will advocate for yourself. Not only will this pave the way for you in future salary conversations, but it will also help you in performance reviews, with setting healthy boundaries, securing a promotion, and more.

Just about all of us could use more money. Perhaps you've been struggling financially or need to pay off some debt. What are a few things you could do if you made more money?

....

....

....

....

With those things in mind (and if you had no fear or hesitancy about doing so), list some reasons why negotiating your salary is important to you:

....

....

....

....

HOW TO RESEARCH SALARY

Before you can negotiate your salary, you have to do some research and figure out two things: your value in the role and your value in the market. Your value in a role is determined by the years of experience you have in your industry and that job title; relevant degrees, skills, coursework, software and/or language expertise; and your achievements in your industry.

To determine your value in the market, ask a few people in your network with similar career experience how much they make. You can also research salaries on websites like payscale.com (fill out the questionnaire) or glassdoor.com.

Also, as you review job listings for your desired title, you'll notice many now include the starting salary or a range. Track how many new listings there are for that position—if there are ten or more per day, that role is in high demand.

After you've done your salary research, you'll use that info to determine the following:

- Your "magic number": This is the salary that excites you, but feels like a bit of a reach.
- Your "reach-for-the-stars" number: Even higher than your magic number, this one feels like a huge reach (at least, right now).
- Your "walk-away" number: This is the absolute minimum amount you would accept.

FIND YOUR MAGIC NUMBER

INTENTION: Research your value in a role and the market to calculate your "magic number."

As you perform your salary research, fill out the chart below (pull your achievements with metrics from your resume).

YEARS OF EXPERIENCE IN ROLE/INDUSTRY	+ RELEVANT SKILLS/ EDUCATION	+ ACHIEVEMENTS WITH METRICS	= YOUR VALUE IN THE ROLE
PAYSCALE.COM QUESTIONNAIRE RESULT	+ COLLECTED SALARY DATA	+ CURRENT DEMAND FOR ROLE	= YOUR MARKET VALUE
AMOUNT OFFERED	YOUR WALK-AWAY NUMBER	YOUR REACH-FOR-THE-STARS NUMBER	YOUR MAGIC NUMBER

GATHERING EVIDENCE TO PROVE YOUR WORTH

Whether you're asking for a raise at your current company or negotiating your salary at a new job, you need to provide objective proof of what you've achieved and contributed.

This is your "business case," and it's straight-up evidence of your badassery. A strong business case includes all of the following:

- **YOUR IMPACT:** Relevant achievements, innovations, and successful projects and initiatives.

- **METRICS:** The amount of money you've made the company, costs you've saved, resources you've preserved, time you've saved, and so on.

- **YOUR INFLUENCE:** People you've trained, collaborations you were part of, and departments you've assisted.

- **EVOLUTION:** How your responsibilities and the scope of your role have grown.

- **ACCOLADES:** Positive feedback you've received from leadership and colleagues.

A business case that includes all of these is just the evidence you need to get what you're worth.

BUILD YOUR BUSINESS CASE

INTENTION: Collect the necessary evidence to get a raise, new job, or promotion.

This template will help you gather your evidence and build your business case. Pull your achievements and metrics from your resume and the salary research template (page 67).

IMPACT	
METRICS	
INFLUENCE	
EVOLUTION	
ACCOLADES	

NEGOTIATING TO GET WHAT YOU'RE WORTH

INTENTION: Get comfortable with taking up space and being heard.

You can role-play the following dialogue with a friend, or video or audio record yourself rehearsing the answers. Note the use of collaborative language ("we" instead of "I" or "you").

Interviewer: We look forward to you joining the team. This position pays

$_____ *per year.*
  [Unacceptable number]

You: "Thank you for the offer. I'm excited about joining the team! Based on my

experience, the value I'm bringing to this role, and my current market rate, I'm

looking for $_____. Can we make that happen?"
              [Your magic number]

Interviewer: Unfortunately, we can't budge on salary.

You: "A sign-on bonus of $_____ and a yearly bonus
                          [Amount to reach magic number]

of $_____ percent would get me closer to my target
    [Amount to reach magic number]

compensation. Is that possible?"

Interviewer: We're pleased to offer you the highly competitive rate of

$_____ *per year.*
  [Unacceptable number]

You: "Thank you. I have a competing offer of $_____,
                                             [Offered amount]

but I'm so excited about this opportunity. Can you match?"

THE POST-NEGOSH DEBRIEF

INTENTION: Reflect and clarify your feelings after a negotiation so you can make an informed decision.

Regardless of the outcome, celebrate the fact that you advocated for yourself and raised the bar for the next person. After each salary negotiation, either write down or video or audio record your answers to the following questions so you'll have a record of your thoughts and feelings:

What surprised you about your salary negotiation conversation?

....

....

....

What went especially well?

....

....

....

What will you would do differently next time?

....

....

....

....

POWER MOOD BOARD

doodle, create, reflect

INTENTION: Express all the methods you've learned to conjure your Power Mood.

What were your most powerful takeaways from Part I: Conjuring? Use the space below to jot notes, draw, or express whatever affected and/or resonated with you the most:

Celebrate What You've Learned

INTENTION: Celebrate the time and effort you've put into this workbook so far, your career, and yourself!

In Part I, you've learned how to craft a compelling resume, interview with finesse, and negotiate for what you're worth. Before you move on, take a moment to celebrate your hard work. Reflect on what you've learned so far on your path to finding your Power Mood and add more of your own at the end:

- You've discovered your superpowers and know how valuable they are.

- You've defined your ideal work environment.

- You have a resume you're proud of that highlights your achievements.

- You're ready to interview confidently and showcase your superpowers.

- You're excited to advocate for yourself in a salary negotiation.

- ....

- ....

- ....

- ....

- ....

- ....

- ....

- ....

You hold the power to craft your experience at work.

PART II: CRAFTING

Congrats on your new job!

   After you've landed that new position, it's time to make an impact, build relationships, and get promoted! In this section, you'll learn all about how to set yourself up for success during the first ninety days of your new job.

   You'll also learn how to set achievable goals and communicate more confidently (and effectively) at work.

   This is the stuff they don't teach you at school, but probably should. There's so much to prepare for, but also so many curveballs that can throw you off.

   In this section, you'll learn and practice actionable strategies to handle all of these situations with confidence and professionalism. When you have an intentional plan going in, it will help you craft your own path to achieve your goals.

CHAPTER 6

Making a Great Impression

Have you ever felt nervous or completely overwhelmed at the thought of starting a brand-new job? Me too! That's why I built a sturdy, intentional game plan for success within the first ninety days.

With a strong plan in place, those first few months can actually feel empowering and deliberate, rather than chaotic and exhausting.

The activities in this chapter will help you create a plan for your first three months, including which questions to ask, agendas to use, what kind of feedback to share, and more.

You'll also learn how to set smart, achievable goals that build a foundation for promotion right out of the gate.

If you focus on what you can control, not only will you enjoy your first few months at a new job, you'll also make an astounding impression.

THE THREE C's

If you create a road map to success for your first ninety days, you'll walk into that new job prepared and confident. When you have an intentional plan from day one, it not only makes you feel more secure, but also helps you establish yourself at your new organization.

Regardless of what they throw at you (or fail to provide you), you'll be able to handle it if you have a plan to center you.

If you keep the following three C's in mind, they'll help you stay on track:

- **CURIOSITY:** Be an active listener and ask strategic questions that showcase your intellect and passion.

- **CONNECTION:** Set up one-on-one meetings with core colleagues and anyone (including leaders) with whom you'll be working cross-functionally. It's important that you get to know them and their communication style, and that they get to know you and your superpowers.

- **CREATION:** As you become accustomed to the systems and processes, you can (and should) thoughtfully weigh in on anything you think can be improved, and how. Also, identify any gaps in your job description and share any ideas you have about refining your role, and how these would positively impact the team.

CURIOSITY, CONNECTION, CREATION

INTENTION: Use the three C's to create a plan for your first ninety days.

Fill out the template below to create an intentional, specific map to success for your first three months at a new job:

	KEY COWORKERS	RECURRING MEETINGS	CORE PROJECTS
CURIOSITY (FIRST 30 DAYS)			
	COWORKER SUPERPOWERS	PREFERRED FORM OF COMMUNICATION	LEADERS TO GET TO KNOW
CONNECTION (FIRST 60 DAYS)			
	ONBOARDING/ TRAINING PROCESS	POTENTIAL IMPROVEMENTS	POTENTIAL JOB DESCRIPTION CHANGES
CREATION (FIRST 90 DAYS)			

YOUR FIRST THIRTY DAYS

INTENTION: Debrief after your first month at a new job.

It's time for a thirty-day check-in! Answer the following questions:

Has anything surprised you? If so, what (be specific)?

....

....

....

What is going particularly well?

....

....

What has been challenging?

....

....

Has leadership been supportive? How have they demonstrated (or not demonstrated) this?

....

....

Can you see yourself growing at this company? Why or why not?

....

....

....

YOUR PROGRESS AFTER ONE MONTH

INTENTION: Note your accomplishments during your first month on the job.

Review the following list and check off those you've accomplished. If there's anything you haven't yet done, add it below and to your calendar for the coming week.

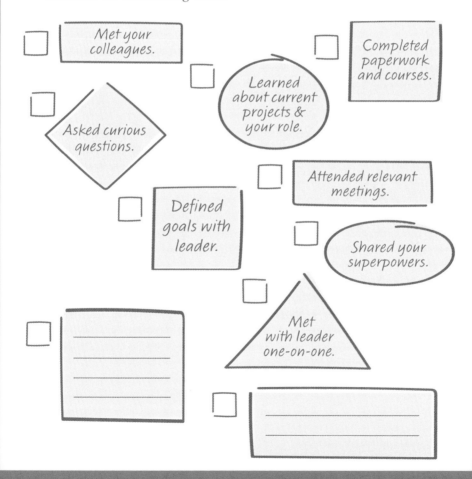

☐ Met your colleagues.

☐ Completed paperwork and courses.

☐ Learned about current projects & your role.

☐ Asked curious questions.

☐ Attended relevant meetings.

☐ Defined goals with leader.

☐ Shared your superpowers.

☐ Met with leader one-on-one.

☐ _____

☐ _____

SMART GOALS

You might have heard the term "SMART goals" before; it stands for the following:

- **S**pecific: The clearer the goal, the easier it is to map out your steps to get there.

- **M**easurable: Like the metrics on your resume, these are your accomplishments in data (percentages, numbers, dollars, and so on).

- **A**chievable: Make sure your goals are actually within reach; for example, increasing attendance to an event by 25 percent, but not 200 percent.

- **R**elevant: Define why and/or how achieving this goal will benefit the team/company.

- **T**ime-Based: Having a timeline will help you prioritize what needs to be completed, and in what order.

A non-SMART goal might look something like this: "Increase attendance at our annual conference."

Here's that same goal made SMART: "Increase attendance at our annual conference (**S**pecific) by 30 percent (**M**easurable). Last year we had 300 guests; goal this year is 390 (**A**chievable). This will increase brand visibility, generate leads, and drive revenue, (**R**elevant). To achieve, we'll send out a series of four targeted marketing emails, starting eight weeks before the conference (**T**ime-based)."

MAKING YOUR GOALS **SMART**

INTENTION: Make your goals Specific, Measurable, Achievable, Relevant, and Time-based.

Now it's your turn! Start by writing a goal as specifically as possible and follow the example on the previous page to fill in the rest of the table.

SPECIFIC	
MEASURABLE	
ACHIEVABLE	
RELEVANT	
TIME-BASED	
SMART GOAL	

YOUR FIRST SIXTY DAYS

INTENTION: Debrief after your first two months at a new job.

Congrats! You've made it through the first sixty days, and it's time for another check-in to gauge how you're feeling about your new gig. Answer the following questions and reflect on your first two months:

Are any of your colleague's superpowers similar to yours? Whose are the most different?

....

....

....

What is going particularly well?

....

....

....

What have you learned about your leader's communication and leadership style? Does it align with your needs? Why or why not?

....

....

....

Have you met anyone who could potentially be a mentor?

....

....

YOUR PROGRESS AFTER TWO MONTHS

INTENTION: Note your accomplishments during your first two months on the job.

Review the following list and check off the items you've accomplished. If there's anything you haven't done yet, add it to your calendar for the coming week.

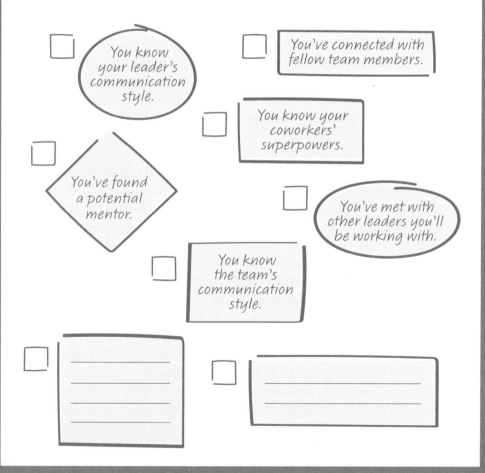

You know your leader's communication style.

You've connected with fellow team members.

You know your coworkers' superpowers.

You've found a potential mentor.

You've met with other leaders you'll be working with.

You know the team's communication style.

WHAT YOU'VE LEARNED

INTENTION: Appreciate how much you've learned in only three months.

The first ninety days at a new job tend to be the toughest because so much is thrown at you, seemingly all at once! Whether you realize it or not, you've grown exponentially. Finish the following prompts to see just how much you've learned and grown in such a short time.

I'm proudest of the following achievements:

....

....

....

I employed my superpowers in the following situations:

....

....

....

I've made connections with the following people:

....

....

....

I've learned and grown in the following ways:

....

....

....

YOUR FIRST NINETY DAYS

INTENTION: Debrief after your first three months at a new job.

Well, you've done it! You made it through the first ninety days at your new job, so you know what that means: it's time for another check-in. Answer the following questions and reflect on your first three months.

How do you feel about the overall training and onboarding experience? What went well and what could have been better?

....

....

....

Have you identified any processes that could be improved and, if so, how would you do it?

....

....

....

Has your job description proven to be accurate thus far? What (if any) changes would you recommend?

....

....

....

CHAPTER 7

Replacing "Sorry" and Other Filler Words

*S*orry about that! Sorry to bug you. Sorry, I'll fix that! Sorry, I'm not sure if that made sense.

Sound familiar? If you tend to say "sorry" countless times every day, you're not alone—especially if you're a woman.

The burden placed on girls at a young age to always be polite becomes an ingrained societal pressure we have to unlearn.

When you eliminate unnecessary apologies (especially when you've done nothing wrong), you release unwarranted self-blame. You'll be amazed at how much doing this one thing can expand your self-worth and confidence.

The activities in this chapter will help you examine your potential overuse of the word "sorry" and other filler words, and replace them with more confident language.

ARE YOU AN OVER-APOLOGIZER?

> **INTENTION:** Examine when and how much you use the word "sorry" and discern if there are any situations in which you can eliminate it.

Over-apologizing not only weakens your confidence, it diminishes the value of the word "sorry." This quiz will help you see where you're at on the "sorry meter" so you can take the appropriate action. Answer the following questions honestly:

1. **If someone bumps into you, you:**
   A. Apologize to them.
   B. Feel embarrassed and don't make eye contact.
   C. Make eye contact, but do and say nothing.

2. **When you make a mistake at work, you:**
   A. Apologize to your boss immediately.
   B. Feel terrible and berate yourself with negative self-talk for days.
   C. Own it and learn from it.

3. **If you're five minutes late to a meeting because the one before it ran long, you:**

   A. Apologize for being late.

   B. Mention that your previous meeting ran over.

   C. Express gratitude for everyone's patience and move forward.

4. **When you need to ask your boss a question, you:**

   A. Apologize first for taking up their time, and then ask.

   B. Are so nervous to approach them and ask, you put it off.

   C. Ask if now is a good time for a question and, if they say yes, you ask away.

5. **When you can't take on another work project because your plate is already full, you:**

   A. Apologize and say you're unable to work on that right now.

   B. Take it on anyway.

   C. Recommend other projects that could be deprioritized so you can work on that one.

6. **Before you share your perspective during a meeting, you:**

A. Often qualify it by saying, "Sorry, I'm not sure if this makes sense, but . . ."

B. Don't typically share during meetings at all.

C. Share your point of view clearly and confidently.

7. **If something goes wrong at work that wasn't your fault, but your boss approaches you about it, you:**

A. Apologize before you've even heard all the details.

B. Get very nervous and stay quiet.

C. Communicate what you know about the situation honestly and directly.

CALCULATE YOUR RESULTS

Mostly A's: Well, sorry (ha!), but you're an over-apologizer. However, the first step to getting better is acknowledging that you have a problem, so taking this quiz means you're well on your way! In the future, work on being more intentional about the situations in which you say "sorry." If you only apologize when it's warranted, you'll avoid feeling needlessly diminished.

Mostly B's: You don't over-apologize, but that's because you don't say much at all. Most likely, you lack confidence in yourself, which puts you at risk for burnout—especially when you don't let your boss know that your plate is overloaded. You're also extremely hard on yourself. Give yourself a break and permission to make mistakes sometimes (that's how we learn, after all). No one is expecting perfection except you, so try to be gentler with yourself and work on speaking up more often.

Mostly C's: No problems here! Your communication style is confident and direct. You're not afraid to take up space and share your ideas, but you also won't accept unnecessary blame and apologize for things that aren't your fault. The only warning here would be to make sure you don't take things too far, and never say you're sorry even when something *is* your fault.

WHEN NOT TO SAY YOU'RE SORRY

INTENTION: Recognize the situations in which "sorry" isn't the right word, so you can refine your communication.

To stop over-apologizing, you first have to recognize the situations in which "sorry" isn't the right word. Review the following list and check off any situations in which you've apologized at work:

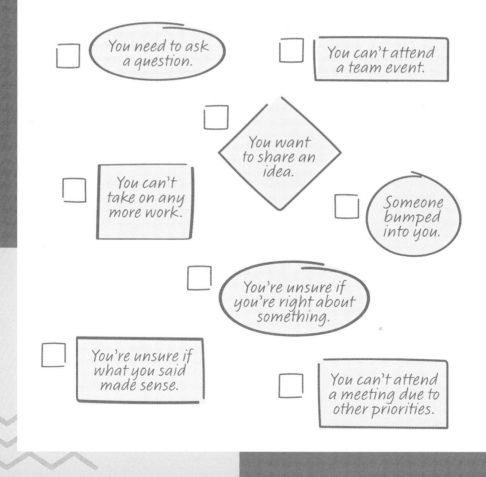

- [ ] You need to ask a question.
- [ ] You can't attend a team event.
- [ ] You want to share an idea.
- [ ] You can't take on any more work.
- [ ] Someone bumped into you.
- [ ] You're unsure if you're right about something.
- [ ] You're unsure if what you said made sense.
- [ ] You can't attend a meeting due to other priorities.

SHOULD YOU EVEN BE SORRY?

INTENTION: Stop taking accountability for (and wasting emotional energy on) things that aren't your fault.

Apologizing expends energy, which is why it's so important to make sure that when you do so, it's warranted and you truly mean it. Hone in on how it makes you feel whenever you apologize.

Take at least one day to count how often you use the word "sorry," both at work and in your personal life, and then respond to the prompts below.

Number of times you said "sorry" today:

....

....

Was an apology truly warranted in each of these situations?

....

....

....

Did you feel relieved or diminished in each of these situations?

....

....

....

REPLACING SORRY

If you're an over-apologizer, you have to consciously unlearn the instinct that makes you instantly say "sorry" for any- and everything. This will take a while to get comfortable with, but whenever you know you're about to apologize, take a beat and remind yourself not to accept unnecessary blame.

The table below provides some simple words and phrases you can say instead of "sorry." Rather than apologizing for something out of your control, simply reframe the sentence without the apology, and use confident, professional language instead. Once you get in the habit of eliminating all those sorries, you'll never look back.

INSTEAD OF THIS:	SAY THIS:
"Sorry, but I'm unable to take that on."	"Is that deadline flexible? I'm currently on deadlines with projects A and B."
"Sorry to bother you, but I have a quick question."	"Is now a good time to ask you a question?"
"Sorry I'm late; my last meeting ran long."	"Thank you for your patience. I'm really looking forward to this discussion."
"Sorry—I really messed that up."	"Thank you for the feedback. I'm on it for next time."
"Sorry, but I disagree."	"I have a different perspective on this."
"Sorry, I'm not sure if this makes sense."	"Let's look at this from a different angle."

PRACTICE NOT SAYING "SORRY"

INTENTION: Explore how it feels when you stop over-apologizing at work.

It will take some time to deprogram the urge to over-apologize. After you've practiced replacing "sorry" for a few days, though, take some time to reflect and answer the following questions:

How does it feel when you don't apologize in situations in which you previously did?

....

....

....

How did others react to you?

....

....

....

In what ways (direct and/or indirect) did it impact your workday?

....

....

....

....

REPLACING "SORRY" AND OTHER FILLER WORDS IN EMAILS

There are a few core elements of an effective email and over-apologizing isn't one of them. It doesn't serve you or the recipient, nor does it get you the answers you need. An effective email contains all of the following information:

- **THE WHY:** The reason why it's important that they respond to you. What is at stake?
- **THE CLEAR ASK:** The precise thing you need from them. Be clear about what and when (use a specific date).
- **EMPATHY:** Instead of "sorry," let them know you're there to help get this task accomplished.
- **GRATITUDE:** Thank them for their attention and for helping to make it happen.

You'll also want to eliminate other filler words, including "just," "totally," "but," "very," "if possible," and anything else that's just taking up space.

Here's an example of an email chock-full of filler words:

Sorry to bug you again! I just wanted to check in on the email I sent on Tuesday regarding Project Purple and make sure you received it? Totally understand that you're very busy right now with everything going on, but just wanted to circle back and see if I could receive this by the end of the week if possible?

Thanks!

WRITE AN EMAIL THAT DELIVERS RESULTS

INTENTION: Learn to replace filler words with confident, direct language in your digital communication so you get what you need.

Just like your speech, sorry and other filler words can creep into your emails and other digital communication, as well. When used excessively, these words can make you appear less knowledgeable about a subject than you really are.

In the space below, rewrite the email on the previous page using confident, direct language. Eliminate all filler words and make sure it contains the why, a clear ask, empathy, and gratitude:

CHAPTER 8

Building Relationships at Work

When it comes to moving up in your career and ensuring your general happiness on the job, building strong working relationships is essential. Not only will it make your life much easier, it is also one of the keys to your success, and it all starts with communication.

You should be intentional about building a relationship with your boss, in particular. This is why scheduling a regular one-on-one meeting with them is a good idea.

It will give you an opportunity to proactively communicate your unique superpowers, and discuss projects you've led, ideas you've had, presentations you've created, and so on.

The activities in this chapter will also help you identify what type of boss you have and define what you value most in a leader.

SUPPORTIVE BOSS BEHAVIORS
(GREEN FLAGS)

INTENTION: Identify the behaviors you value most in a leader.

Think about the kind of boss who allows you to do your best work. What type of boss inspires you and makes you feel most at ease? If you've had leaders in the past who have been impactful in a good way, consider those traits.

Review the following behaviors and check off at least five that are the most important to you in a potential boss, then add a few of your own:

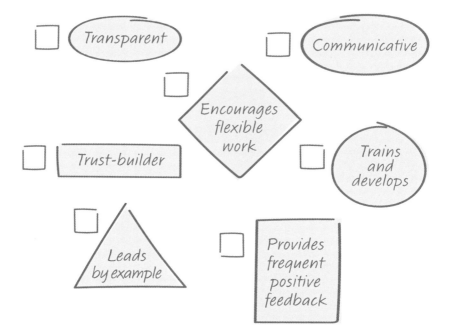

☐ Transparent

☐ Communicative

☐ Encourages flexible work

☐ Trust-builder

☐ Trains and develops

☐ Leads by example

☐ Provides frequent positive feedback

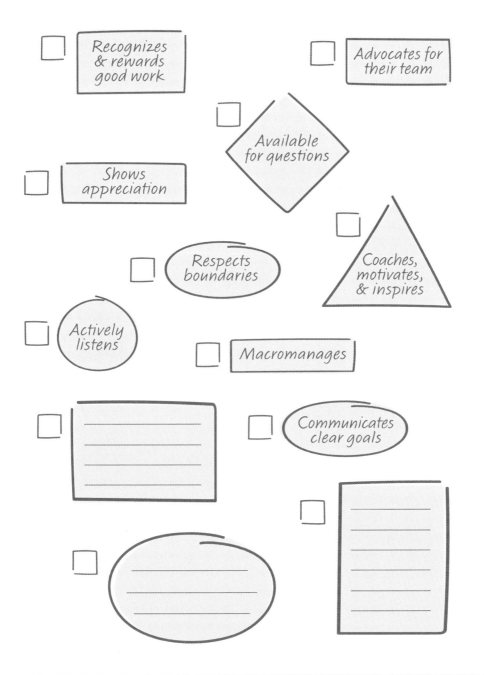

☐ Recognizes & rewards good work

☐ Advocates for their team

☐ Available for questions

☐ Shows appreciation

☐ Respects boundaries

☐ Coaches, motivates, & inspires

☐ Actively listens

☐ Macromanages

☐ _____

☐ Communicates clear goals

☐ _____

☐ _____

WHAT IS A "TOXIC" BOSS?

The term "toxic boss" is quite common in modern workplace culture, but what does it really mean? Some of the more obvious signs you have a toxic boss include the following:

- They only give constructive and/or negative feedback, never positive.
- They are combative, put you down, and/or regularly make you jump through hoops.
- They are sexist, racist, and/or intolerant.
- They pile work on you when you're already over capacity.
- They micromanage, bully, or harass you.
- They play favorites.
- They take credit for your work, but blame you for their failures.

While the following behaviors are less obvious than the list above, they're still signs of a toxic boss:

- They have unrealistic expectations.
- They don't respect your boundaries.
- They seem threatened by you.
- They don't advocate for you when it comes to promotions and raises.

THE TOXIC BOSS INCIDENT LOG

INTENTION: Document all toxic behavior you are subjected to from your boss so you have a record if you need it (to present to human resources, pursue legal action, and so on).

When toxic incidents occur, you likely forget about them as time passes. That's why it's important to be intentional and write them down. If you're dealing with a toxic boss, use the template below to log all incidents of this behavior.

DATE	LOCATION OF DOCS/EMAILS	WHAT HAPPENED & HOW YOU FELT

IS YOUR BOSS SUPPORTIVE, TOXIC, OR IN-BETWEEN?

> **INTENTION:** Identify what type of leader you have so you know how to proceed.

Bosses come in all varieties; the best are supportive and the worst are toxic, but many are somewhere in-between. To discover which kind you have, respond to each question below by circling A, B, or C:

1. **Your regular one-on-one meetings with your boss consist of:**
   A. We don't have regular one-on-ones.
   B. Project status updates.
   C. Status updates, any questions I have, short-term goals check-in, and long-term development discussion.

2. **Before assigning you additional work or projects, your boss:**
   A. Simply assigns you the work.
   B. Asks you when you would be able to have it completed.
   C. Checks in with you about your current workload to see if you have the capacity to take on something else.

3. **Rate your level of agreement with this statement: "I know exactly what my boss expects of me. They set clear expectations and articulate consistent goals."**
   A. Strongly disagree
   B. Mostly agree
   C. Strongly agree

4. **When you bring up the subject of a promotion to your boss, they:**

   A. Deny you without reason, feel threatened, or brush off the conversation.

   B. Support you in the initial meeting, but never follow up with you about it.

   C. Are supportive and help you develop an action plan and timeline to reach your goal.

5. **After you deliver excellent work, your boss responds by:**

   A. Not acknowledging it at all, or taking credit for it themselves.

   B. Complimenting you via email or in-person.

   C. Sharing specific, positive feedback with you in a one-on-one *and* recognizing your work publicly in a team meeting.

6. **When it comes to overseeing your work, which of the following best describes your boss?**

   A. Extreme micromanager. Wants to be copied on all of your emails, consulted on all of your business decisions, and involved in every meeting.

   B. Moderate micromanager. Occasionally interferes with your work, periodically makes edits to your emails, but usually allows a degree of freedom and flexibility.

   C. Macromanager. Trusts you to deliver great work *your* way, allows you to make business decisions on your own, but provides support when you need it.

QUIZ

7. **Which of the following best describes how you feel when you approach your boss to ask a work-related question?**
   A. Afraid: They intimidate you and keep themselves extremely busy. It's usually impossible to even track them down to ask a question.
   B. Cautious. When you do ask a question, it typically takes them a very long time to respond.
   C. Confident. They've made it clear they're available as a resource, and they often respond quickly.

8. **How many people has your boss developed and promoted in the last year?**
   A. A. 0
   B. B. 1–2
   C. C. 3+

9. **Which of the following best describes your boss's communication style?**
   A. Combative and/or defensive
   B. Warm and casual
   C. Supportive and empathetic

10. **Which of the following best describes how often, and the manner in which, your boss delivers feedback?**
    A. Rarely. Mostly constructive, but without any specific examples or a growth plan.
    B. Fairly frequently. A mix of positive and constructive, but without any specific examples or a growth plan.
    C. Regularly. More positive than constructive, with specific behavioral examples, and a growth plan for the future that targets areas of opportunity.

CALCULATE YOUR RESULTS

Mostly A's: I'm sorry to say you have a toxic boss on your hands. These types of bosses simply manage, they don't lead. Their approach is also usually harsh and combative, and they certainly won't advocate for you. I strongly encourage you to start documenting their behavior and don't wait until you fill an entire notebook to do something about it—you deserve better! All you'll learn from this type of boss is what *not* to do as a leader.

Mostly B's: Your boss falls somewhere in-between supportive and toxic, meaning they're neutral. They aren't downright awful, but they also don't advocate for your growth and success. They provide the bare minimum when it comes to leadership.

Mostly C's: Congratulations! Your boss is supportive. They set clear expectations, check in with you regularly about your goals and development, and vocally advocate for you to help you achieve your career goals. This is a boss from whom you can learn.

DEALING WITH A MICROMANAGER

At their core, micromanagers lack trust and think no one can do a job as well as they can. As a result, they keep a hawk eye on their team's every email, project, and decision.

However, asking curious questions and being direct about how their constant oversight is preventing you from succeeding is an effective way to handle them.

Below are some questions you can ask to deal with your micromanaging manager:

- "Are you concerned about the quality of my work? If so, can you please provide examples?"

- "I work best when I have a degree of freedom over my work. Can we work toward that?"

- "I deliver my best when I work independently. Can we take steps toward this?"

- "Can we set up a specific time each week for updates?"

When all else fails, and if it's feasible, you might want to ask human resources to transfer you to another manager.

IDENTIFYING A MICROMANAGER

INTENTION: Discover if your boss is a micromanager so you can create an action plan and deal with them effectively.

This is one of the worst of the toxic bosses, but before you can deal effectively with one, you have to know how to spot them! Below are some behavioral signs of a micromanager; check off all those that apply to your boss:

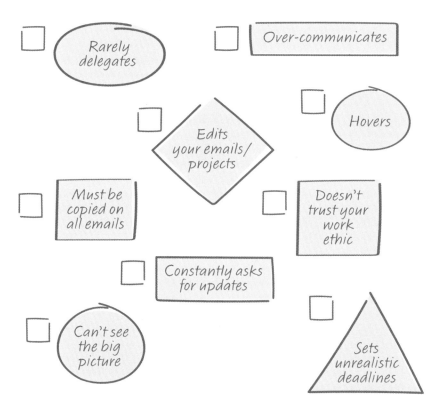

- ☐ Rarely delegates
- ☐ Over-communicates
- ☐ Hovers
- ☐ Edits your emails/projects
- ☐ Must be copied on all emails
- ☐ Doesn't trust your work ethic
- ☐ Constantly asks for updates
- ☐ Can't see the big picture
- ☐ Sets unrealistic deadlines

HOW TO BE AN ALLY IN THE WORKPLACE

Maybe you don't have to deal with a toxic manager, but you regularly witness them subjecting others to their negative behavior. Perhaps you've even noticed your workplace lacks equity in terms of pay and position when it comes to women and people of color. It's important to call attention to these issues and prevent them from continuing to happen.

Below are some concrete ways you can be more supportive of your coworkers:

- **Call out harassment and discrimination in the moment:** Never be a silent bystander and always report any incident.

- **Give credit where credit is due:** Point out when someone's ideas and contributions have made a difference on a project, especially if someone else tries to take credit.

- **Notice who isn't in the meeting:** If there are zero women or people of color at the conference table, call this out and make suggestions to change it.

- **Encourage men to take on office housework duties:** Guys can also make coffee, organize team events, or take notes during a meeting.

- **If you're in a leadership role, mentor women and people of color:** Do what you can to help them advance by giving them special projects, clients, or assignments.

ARE YOU A WORKPLACE ALLY?

INTENTION: Discover if you're doing all you can to assist any coworkers who may be at a disadvantage.

If you're in a leadership position now (or in the future), it's important to be aware of moments where you can be an ally to those subjected to discrimination, or a lack of equity when it comes to pay and opportunities.

Answer the following questions based on what you've done in the past, or what you would do in the situation described:

1. **During a meeting, if someone interrupts someone else, you:**
   A. Do nothing.
   B. Are usually the one interrupting.
   C. Say something like, "I don't think she was finished speaking."

2. **If you witness harassment in the workplace, you:**
   A. Do nothing in the moment, but check afterward to make sure the person is okay.
   B. Do nothing. It's not your problem.
   C. Call out the behavior in the moment as "not okay," and check in with the person being harassed.

QUIZ

3. **If you need a six-person team to work on a large, highly visible project, you:**

   A. Choose the top six performers on the team.

   B. Choose your six favorite coworkers.

   C. Choose based on the superpowers you need for the project and ensure it's a diverse group.

4. **When it comes to informal feedback for your peers, you:**

   A. Provide it only when asked and offer minimal details.

   B. Offer it unsolicited.

   C. Provide it when asked and include specific examples.

5. **If everyone was expected to pitch in on office housework duties, you would:**

   A. Help out when asked.

   B. Never have time—you're just too busy!

   C. Pitch in when you can without being asked.

6. **If someone takes credit for someone else's idea/work in a meeting, you:**

   A. Ask the person who came up with the idea/did the work how they feel about what happened after the meeting.

   B. Do nothing.

   C. Immediately say something like, "Didn't Rosa initiate that project? Can we get her perspective?"

7. **Which three words would you use to describe an outspoken colleague?**

   A. Confident, direct, and clear.

   B. Aggressive, intimidating, and bossy.

   C. Ambitious, leader, and courageous.

CALCULATE YOUR RESULTS

Mostly A's: You're on your way to becoming a much-needed advocate and ally in the workplace. You just need to break out of your comfort zone a bit more and show up in the moment for colleagues who need your support. A huge part of being an ally is speaking up, so make more of an effort to call out any harassment, bias, or discrimination when it happens.

Mostly B's: You have a bit of a journey ahead of you, but it can be done! First, take an objective look at your own behavior—how would you feel if someone subjected you to the same? With that in mind, try to be a bit more empathetic, especially in your communication. Also, be on the lookout for moments when you can advocate for others. Take action in the moment if you witness any harassment, bias, or discrimination.

Mostly C's: You are a reliable workplace ally! You always make an effort to be supportive and speak up if you witness discrimination, harassment, or bias. There's always more learning and unlearning to do, but your gut instinct to advocate for others is evident and serving you well. Keep going and look deeper at things like workplace policies, rules, or processes, where perhaps some fundamental changes could improve things even further.

CHAPTER 9

Tactical Ambition

Tactical ambition means taking specific actions in order to secure a promotion. In the corporate world, you have to play the game and advocate for yourself. Doing excellent work simply isn't enough, especially if you're a woman and/or person of color.

That's why you need some tools to hack the corporate system! Self-advocacy is essential: Share your accomplishments with leadership, quantify them, and make your impact on the business known.

Of course, this is easier said than done because self-advocacy takes practice and requires confidence.

The activities in this chapter will help you unlock the tools you need to build a sturdy, confident foundation, so you can effectively deploy tactical ambition and get that promotion.

THE BRAG SHEET

When you're in the thick of your daily routine, it's easy to forget about your stellar contributions. That's why a brag sheet is a necessity!

This ongoing list of all your notable achievements will really come in handy when you have a job interview, need to update your resume, or when it's time to advocate for a raise or promotion.

Your brag sheet should contain all of the following:

- **YOUR SUPERPOWERS**: The things you are better at than anyone else (see Chapter 2).
- **YOUR ACHIEVEMENTS**: Meetings you've led, presentations you've created, deadlines you've hit, and so on.
- **LEADERSHIP FEEDBACK**: Positive feedback you've received from higher-ups.
- **PEER FEEDBACK**: Positive feedback from your colleagues.

If you haven't yet received any feedback from your boss or peers, ask for it! Shoot them an email and ask how you did on that task, project, or presentation. This way, you'll have their responses documented in two places: your email and on your brag sheet.

It's never too late to start a brag sheet, so start jotting down those wins!

START YOUR BRAG SHEET

INTENTION: Keep track of all of your accomplishments in one place.

If you don't yet have a brag sheet, it's time to get going! Jot down all your most recent accomplishments on the template below, and then set a reminder to update it weekly.

ACHIEVEMENT	
LEADERSHIP FEEDBACK	
PEER FEEDBACK	
ACHIEVEMENT	
LEADERSHIP FEEDBACK	
PEER FEEDBACK	
ACHIEVEMENT	
LEADERSHIP FEEDBACK	
PEER FEEDBACK	

IDEAS THAT INFLUENCE

INTENTION: Get in the habit of coming up with influential ideas to boost your presence at work.

An idea is influential when it directly serves your predetermined goals, broader company goals, or both. Use the prompts below to construct three ideas, including how they will contribute toward achieving a goal, and then present them to your boss at your next one-on-one.

Idea 1: How to improve an existing process:

....

....

....

Idea 2: Create a new process to solve a problem:

....

....

....

Idea 3: Propose a new tool, program, or software that solves a problem/helps reach a goal:

....

....

....

DEVELOP A PLAN FOR PROMOTION

INTENTION: Create a clear plan to prepare for your next position.

If you want to move up in your company, the first step is to discuss it with your boss at your next one-on-one. Find out which specific skills you need to develop, the timeline, the people you need to connect with to make it happen, and how your success will be measured. Fill out this template to create a concrete plan for your promotion.

SKILLS TO DEVELOP	
TIMELINE	
KEY PEOPLE	
HOW SUCCESS WILL BE MEASURED	

WHAT IS A BUSINESS CASE?

A business case is evidence of your worth. It backs up whatever you're asking for (like that promotion or raise) and helps ensure that you get it! A strong business case includes the facts and metrics about your top work-related achievements. Essentially, it shows the impact you've had on the business.

To start building your business case, gather all of the following information:

- **YOUR ACHIEVEMENTS WITH METRICS:** Your accomplishment with supporting numbers and details, such as, "Trained and developed four new team members on core tech systems and signature hospitality cornerstones."

- **SHORT-TERM IMPACT:** Positive results or feedback you received during the project or immediately after. For example, "Received positive feedback from new hires about the ease and detail of the training process."

- **LONG-TERM IMPACT:** How your achievement positively affected the department, company, or both. For example, "New hires were well prepped to support our guests; one received employee of the month their second month."

- **YEARS OF EXPERIENCE:** How long you've been working professionally in this area.

After you build your business case, be sure to keep it updated. This will ensure you're always prepared to ask for a raise, interview for a new job, or go for that promotion.

BUILD YOUR BUSINESS CASE

INTENTION: Start tracking your achievements, metrics, and impact to make your case for a promotion and/or raise.

Now it's time to build your own business case! Use the Brag Sheet you started earlier in this chapter to fill out the following table.

ACHIEVEMENT W/METRICS	
SHORT-TERM IMPACT	
LONG-TERM IMPACT	
YEARS OF EXPERIENCE	

POWER MOOD BOARD

doodle, create, reflect

INTENTION: Jot notes, draw, or freewrite about where you are in your career, if you want to stay there, or where you want to go next.

Now that you've completed Part II: Crafting, you're armed with all the tools you need to take the next step in your career, whatever you want that to be. Use this space to plan next steps, draw a flow chart of your path to promotion, or anything else you're inspired to scribble.

Celebrate Your Achievements

INTENTION: Inhabit your Power Mood and celebrate your wins.

Now that all of your achievements are fresh in your mind, it's time to pause and reflect on how far you've come! Follow the prompts below and celebrate your accomplishments.

List some of your recent achievements below and note how accomplishing each of them made you feel:

....

....

....

What other goals did you reach based on your achievements?

....

....

....

How did each of your achievements benefit the team/company?

....

....

....

Cultivate your ideal work environment by setting boundaries.

PART III: CULTIVATING

In this final section, you will learn how to recognize and combat the much talked-about imposter syndrome, how to effectively handle conflict, and set boundaries at work. As always, there is a foundation of self-advocacy rooted in all of these concepts.

The activities in this section are a bit more introspective. They'll give you a chance to examine your feelings about things like workplace conflict, maintaining boundaries, and the kind of leader you want to be.

You'll also become a pro at identifying during the interview process whether a company values work-life balance, violates employee boundaries, or doesn't cultivate people-first leadership.

CHAPTER 10

Fighting Imposter Syndrome

Whenever you find yourself doubting your abilities, questioning or diminishing your accomplishments, or feeling like a fraud, you have a case of imposter syndrome. The more you talk about it, the less power it will have.

First though, you have to recognize where imposter syndrome comes from: A society that repeatedly tells you that you aren't good enough.

If you've grown up without seeing yourself represented in the boardroom, you might start to believe that you can't ever get there. This is why it's vital to always remember that you wouldn't be in any room if you didn't belong there.

Everyone experiences imposter syndrome from time to time, but if your case is more all-consuming, the strategies in this chapter will help you push past it and find your Power Mood!

DO YOU HAVE IMPOSTER SYNDROME?

INTENTION: Discover if you have imposter syndrome so you can combat it.

Imposter syndrome is when you don't believe you deserve or have earned your wins or successes, and everyone experiences it to some degree. To find out if you're suffering from a case of imposter syndrome, respond to each statement below by circling True or False:

1. **You struggle to accept compliments:**
   A. True
   B. False

2. **You hold yourself to an incredibly high standard:**
   A. True
   B. False

3. **You fear making mistakes:**
   A. True
   B. False

4. **You downplay your accomplishments and give the credit to others:**
   A. True
   B. False

5. **Whenever you achieve a win, you feel like you didn't earn it:**
   A. True
   B. False

6. **You frequently compare yourself to others:**
   A. True
   B. False

7. **You regularly engage in negative self-talk:**
   A. True
   B. False

8. **You often take on extra work without being asked to go "above and beyond."**
   A. True
   B. False

QUIZ

9. **You don't apply for a job unless you meet every single requirement:**

    A. True

    B. False

10. **You set extremely challenging goals for yourself and feel like a failure when you fall short:**

    A. True

    B. False

CALCULATE YOUR RESULTS

If you circled 1 to 3 A's: You're experiencing "imposter syndrome lite," which is actually pretty normal. However, now that you're aware of it, you can implement the antidotes covered next to banish the few symptoms you have as soon as possible!

If you circled 4 to 6 A's: The bad news is you do, indeed, have imposter syndrome. But the good news is, if you start implementing the antidotes right away, you can start your recovery! Review all the statements you answered as "true," and keep them in mind as you go through the rest of this chapter. The antidotes can help transform your perspective and boost your confidence.

If you circled 7 to 10 A's: This will be a very important chapter for you, my friend, because you're in the throes of a very serious case of imposter syndrome. You are incredibly hard on yourself and hold yourself to an impossible standard. Focus on the antidotes on the following page and implement all of them daily. Unfortunately, this is not an overnight process—you have to retrain your brain. However, like anything else, the more you consciously combat these negative thoughts and feelings, the easier and more natural it will become.

IMPOSTER SYNDROME ANTIDOTES

Now that you know how severe your case of imposter syndrome is, it's time to take action and obliterate it! Doing all of the following will help you get through to the other side.

- **UPDATE YOUR BRAG SHEET (OR START ONE):** Review it whenever you're experiencing self-doubt to remind yourself of everything you've accomplished.

- **GIVE YOURSELF PERMISSION TO BE IN YOUR FEELINGS AND NAME THEM:** Feel like you don't deserve something? Talk out the "why." It's likely due to a super-high standard you only apply to yourself.

- **NEGATIVE THOUGHTS AREN'T FACTS:** When they creep in, remind yourself who you are, and how hard you've worked to get where you are.

- **QUIT THE COMPARISON GAME:** Your journey is yours, and it's not replicable. And keep in mind that what we observe of someone else's life often has very little to do with what's actually happening.

- **TALK TO A TRUSTED FRIEND, FAMILY MEMBER, AND/OR THERAPIST:** Don't suffer in silence. Talking is healing because it can bring validation.

It can be difficult to change negative thought patterns, especially if our perception of the world seems to reinforce them. However, it can be done, and the first step is to eliminate those negative thoughts altogether.

POSITIVE AFFIRMATIONS

INTENTION: Eliminate imposter syndrome by changing negative thoughts to positive.

Positive affirmations are a fantastic (and easy) way to actively combat imposter syndrome. Say all of the following out loud as you strike a power pose, then add some of your own to help you fully inhabit your Power Mood:

- "I am powerful."

- "I am successful."

- "I inspire people through my work."

- "I am getting better every day."

- "Confidence is a choice, and today I choose to be confident."

- "I am worthy of what I desire."

- "I am enough."

- "I am allowed to make mistakes."

- "I have what it takes to achieve my goals."

- "Rejection is protection."

- "My opinion matters."

- "I am proud of who I am and what I bring to the table."

- ....

- ....

- ....

CHAPTER 11

Handling Conflict

Workplace conflict gets a bad reputation. It isn't pleasant, but it serves an important function—it encourages us to engage in dialogue and make decisions that move things forward. If you want to move up at work, it's key to get comfy with conflict, because the higher you rise, the more conflict you'll be engaged in.

Conflict can be healthy, as long as all parties are respectful. When faced with conflict, there are strategies you can employ to make the discussion productive.

When deciding whether or not to engage in conflict, consider how invested you are in the outcome. If you feel strongly about it, use it as an opportunity to advocate for yourself, your team, or your idea. It's a great way to build confidence and inhabit your Power Mood.

WHICH TYPE OF CONFLICT ARE YOU FACING?

To deal with conflict in a healthy way, you first have to identify which type you're experiencing. In her book, *HBR Guide to Dealing with Conflict*, author Amy Gallo described the four types of conflict:

- **Task-related:** What needs to be done?
- **Process-related:** How does it need to be done?
- **Status-related:** Who needs to do it?
- **Relationship-related:** When it gets personal.

When emotions run high, utilize this list to make the conflict-resolution process more objective:

- **Define the conflict:** Identify the core issue that needs to be resolved.
- **Define the desired outcome:** This is the ultimate goal your team is trying to achieve. Often, individual goals can interfere with this and may need to be adjusted.
- **Identify the short-term goal:** The first thing that needs to happen before the entire team can move on to the ultimate goal.
- **Identify the long-term goal:** The ultimate goal the team can go for after the the short-term goal is reached. This may be the same as the desired outcome.
- **Brainstorm ideas:** Invite everyone to share any ideas they have for reaching the short- and long-term goals. The person taking the meeting notes should also include everyone's name next to their idea.
- **Decide which ideas are the most practical:** Most likely, you won't have the resources or budget to enact every suggested idea, so now it's time to narrow down your list to the ideas that are the most feasible.

HOW DO YOU FEEL ABOUT CONFLICT?

INTENTION: Discover how you react to and deal with conflict.

Respond to the questions below to explore how conflict affects you.

How does the idea of conflict make you feel?

....

....

....

Which type(s) of conflict as outlined on the previous page stresses you out the most, and why?

....

....

....

If you have the choice to engage in conflict or not, what do you do?

....

....

....

When you've dealt with conflict in the past, how have you responded?

....

....

....

EFFECTIVE BRAINSTORMING

INTENTION: Come up with an actionable solution to resolve conflict as quickly as possible.

Make copies of this activity and keep them in your desk drawer. Whenever you have an issue to resolve, take one with you to your brainstorming session and respond to the following prompts:

1. What is the problem?

2. What is the desired outcome?

3. What short-term goal does this outcome align with?

4. What long-term goal does this outcome align with?

....

....

....

....

....

....

5. Brainstorm ideas to solve the problem (write each person's name next to their idea).

....

....

....

....

....

....

6. Which potential solutions are the most practical?

....

....

....

....

....

....

IMPLEMENTING THE SOLUTION

After you come up with a solution, it's time to implement it! A solution-tracker model can shepherd you through the conflict resolution process.

The most helpful solution tracker should contain all of the following info:

- **KEY STAKEHOLDERS**: The people who will be involved in implementing the solution.

- **ACTION PLAN**: Write out the plan to implement the solution and obtain that outcome. Include any necessary technology, budgets, processes, and so on.

- **SOLUTION STATEMENT**: The best possible outcome after you implement the solution. It might look something like this, "The best way to achieve our goal is to implement X (the new process or procedure)."

- **IMPLEMENT THE SOLUTION AND TRACK RESULTS**: Be sure someone is in charge of updating progress consistently.

Conflict can feel like chaos when it happens, but now that you have a plan, you've broken the issue down into manageable pieces.

Always keep in mind that healthy conflict in the workplace is standard procedure. Also, identifying problems and fixing them is a superpower, so don't forget to add any issues you resolve to your brag sheet.

SOLUTION TRACKER

INTENTION: Keep track of the progress after you implement a solution to resolve a problem.

Use the table below to track the progress of solutions you implement to solve problems.

KEY STAKEHOLDERS	
ACTION PLAN	
SOLUTION STATEMENT	
DATE & PROGRESS	
DATE & PROGRESS	
DATE & PROGRESS	
DATE & PROGRESS	

CHAPTER 12

Identifying and Setting Healthy Boundaries at Work

Millennials and Gen Zers are at the forefront of the conversation when it comes to setting healthy boundaries in the workplace because they want to lead balanced, fulfilling lives. As a result, they're asking more of their employers than past generations.

They're also putting boundaries in place to ensure that work doesn't take over their entire lives. To some, this seems like a bold, selfish move, but to them, it seems like respecting boundaries is the *bare minimum* a company can do.

Identifying, setting, and maintaining workplace boundaries is one of the best things you can do for yourself. They will not only benefit your career, but also your personal life, mental health, and overall well-being. If you're a consummate people-pleaser, this chapter is essential for you!

HOW DO YOU FEEL ABOUT BOUNDARIES?

INTENTION: Figure out how you feel about boundaries, including what you need, any fears you have about expressing them, and what excites you about the process.

Now more than ever, the conversation around workplace boundaries is front and center. Employees want and deserve a better work-life balance and good employers are responding in kind.

However, not everyone is comfortable with setting boundaries, nor do they even know what boundaries they need to set. This exercise will help you uncover some of your feelings about boundaries so you can proceed to the next phase: setting some!

Answer the following questions:

What fears do you have about setting boundaries?

....

....

....

....

....

....

....

What excites you about setting boundaries?

What boundaries have you already set at work?

What boundaries do you want to set at work?

TYPES OF BOUNDARIES

When you hear the word "boundaries," what comes to mind? There are actually several different types of personal boundaries:

- **PHYSICAL:** This is the level of physical contact (if any) you're okay with. For example, maybe you're cool with handshakes, but not hugs.

- **EMOTIONAL:** This involves detaching your feelings from those of others, and what you feel comfortable sharing about your personal life.

- **COMMUNICATION:** How you prefer to receive work-related information (email, Slack, phone calls, and so on).

- **TIME:** Your workdays and hours.

- **WORKLOAD:** To define this boundary, you have to know where your role starts and ends, and what your optimal workload looks like. For example, which duties do not fall under your job description? Is one project a month enough, or do you prefer more?

Setting workplace boundaries is necessary in every industry and every role. Even if you work for an organization that you trust, it's still imperative to draw a line in certain areas. You should also never apologize for having boundaries. After all, even a job you love isn't worth sacrificing your mental health!

DEFINING YOUR
WORKPLACE BOUNDARIES

INTENTION: Think about what makes you feel comfortable and uncomfortable at work and set personal boundaries.

Like anything else, when you put your boundaries in writing, it makes them seem more official. It will also make it easier for you to communicate and enforce them.

CATAGORY	YOUR BOUNDARIES
PHYSICAL	
EMOTIONAL	
COMMUNICATION	
TIME	
WORKLOAD	

SIGNS A COMPANY WON'T RESPECT YOUR BOUNDARIES

> **INTENTION:** Identify a boundary-violating company during the interview process or within your first ninety days.

If a company is going to continuously cross (or outright ignore) your boundaries, it's important that you spot the signs during the interview process or as early as possible. Check off any of the following boundary-crossing signs that you've noticed during a recent interview or at your current job:

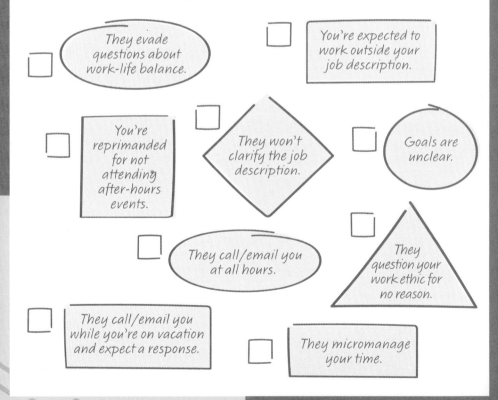

They evade questions about work-life balance.

You're expected to work outside your job description.

You're reprimanded for not attending after-hours events.

They won't clarify the job description.

Goals are unclear.

They call/email you at all hours.

They question your work ethic for no reason.

They call/email you while you're on vacation and expect a response.

They micromanage your time.

COMMUNICATING BOUNDARIES AT WORK

INTENTION: Getting comfortable with boundary-specific phrases.

Now, let's build up some confidence with boundary-setting communication. Practice saying these phrases out loud so you can get used to what it feels like. It might be tough at first, but wait and see— soon, it will be incredibly empowering and you'll never look back.

You can audio or video record yourself saying these, or ask a friend or family member to enact or say the provoking item:

BOUNDARY-CROSSING ACTION	YOUR RESPONSE
Someone goes in for an unwanted hug.	*"I'm more comfortable with this,"* (present your hand for a shake).
Someone asks you a personal question.	*"I prefer not to talk about that at work."*
Someone schedules a meeting at the time your workday ends.	*Politely decline the meeting and suggest an alternative date/time.*
Your boss assigns you more work when your plate is full.	*"Could you help me deprioritize some of these other projects if this one is urgent?"*
Someone asks for your phone number.	*"I prefer email; it's the best way to reach me."*

CHAPTER 13

People-First Leadership

Everyone who has ever had a toxic boss knows all too well that people skills are *essential* to being a good leader. Unfortunately, because many people get promoted based on their technical skills for a job, they don't always have the necessary people skills to effectively lead a team.

A people-first leader intentionally builds trust, consciously cultivates a safe space, recognizes their team's individual strengths, regularly celebrates wins, facilitates growth, and elevates their team to the next level via vocal advocacy.

A good leader always lays out the red carpet to usher in more great leaders; they don't padlock the door.

This chapter's activities will help you unlock your leadership style and non-negotiables, as well as learn to advocate for your team and build a new generation of excellent bosses.

YOUR LEADERSHIP STYLE AND NON-NEGOTIABLES

INTENTION: Identify your leadership style, non-negotiables, and learn what *not* to do.

Becoming an excellent people-first leader starts with incorporating traits you've admired in bosses from your past. Your non-negotiables are the top three things (timeliness, communication, honesty, and so on) that you expect from your team daily, and it's essential that you share this list with them.

Respond to the prompts below to discover your leadership style:

Write down at least four personality traits (kindness, humor, transparency, and so on) that you value most and aim to exude as a leader—this is your leadership style:

....

....

....

....

What are the top three things (your non-negotiables) that you expect from your team daily?

....

....

....

....

TRACKING THE PROGRESS OF YOUR TEAM

INTENTION: Track the growth of each member of your team so you'll know when they're ready for the next step up.

One of the hallmarks of a people-first leader is advocating for their team and promoting from within. This template can help you keep track of everyone's progress.

NAME/TITLE/ DATE OF HIRE	KEY PROJECTS/ AREAS OF OWNERSHIP	NEXT STEPS/ PROMOTION TIMELINE

POWER MOOD BOARD

doodle, create, reflect

INTENTION: Reflect on what you plan to cultivate from Part III.

Use this space to jot down or doodle some your favorite affirmations, your new workplace boundaries, your personal leadership style, and anything else that resonated most with you from Part III: Cultivating.

Celebrate and Embrace Your Power Mood

INTENTION: Reflect on everything you've learned in this workbook.

You've gotten hands-on with combating imposter syndrome, setting your boundaries, and exploring your leadership style, and that's Part III—and this workbook—complete! Congrats on investing in your self-growth.

Hopefully you've arrived on the other side with more clarity and confidence about who you are and feel ready to advocate for yourself in your career—and your life! Respond to the following prompts to see how far you've come.

Previously, my view on imposter syndrome was:

....

....

After completing this section, my view on imposter syndrome has changed in the following ways:

....

....

Previously, my view on workplace conflict was:

....

....

After completing this section, my view on workplace conflict has changed in the following ways:

....

....

....

Previously, my view on workplace boundaries was:

....

....

....

After completing this section, my view on workplace boundaries has changed in the following ways:

....

....

....

Previously, my view on self-advocacy at work was:

....

....

....

After completing this section, my view on self-advocacy at work has changed in the following ways:

....

....

....

ACKNOWLEDGMENTS

This workbook would not have been possible without the support of the Power Mood online community. Thank you for believing in my work! To my LGBTQ+ chosen family and community, thank you for uplifting me and being a soft place to land. A massive shout-out to all the girlies—this one's for you!

To the team at Quarto, especially Rage, Lydia, and Amanda: it's a continued honor to work with such a talented team of inspiring women. Thank you to my literary agent, Rachel Cone-Gorham, for your know-how and encouragement, and thank you to the *Las Culturistas* podcast for being my main source of entertainment during the writing process.

And thanks to everyone who read this far—stay powerful!

ABOUT THE AUTHOR

Sam DeMase is a career-confidence coach and self-advocacy expert. She is also the author of the companion to this workbook, *Power Mood*. Known for her direct, actionable tips on hacking the corporate system, Sam has a community of over 400,000 followers on social media (@apowermood on Instagram). When she's not fighting the patriarchy, you can find her sipping green tea at home in Brooklyn, N.Y., seeing every Broadway musical, and blasting '90s pop divas.

ALSO AVAILABLE:

Power Mood

Unlock Your Confidence, Transform Your Life & Command Your Value

978-1-63106-935-2

First published in 2023 by Rock Point, an imprint of The Quarto Group,
142 West 36th Street, 4th Floor, New York, NY 10018, USA
T (212) 779-4972 F (212) 779-6058 www.Quarto.com

Rock Point titles are also available at discount for retail, wholesale, promotional, and bulk
purchase. For details, contact the Special Sales Manager by email at specialsales@quarto.
com or by mail at The Quarto Group, Attn: Special Sales Manager, 100 Cummings Center
Suite 265D, Beverly, MA 01915 USA.

10 9 8 7 6 5 4 3 2 1

ISBN: 978-1-63106-936-9

Publisher: Rage Kindelsperger
Creative Director: Laura Drew
Managing Editor: Cara Donaldson
Editor: Amanda Gambill
Cover and Interior Design: Kim Winscher

Printed in China

This book provides general information on various widely known and widely accepted
self-help concepts that tend to evoke feelings of strength and confidence. However, it
should not be relied upon as recommending or promoting any specific diagnosis or
method of treatment for a particular condition, and it is not intended as a substitute for
medical advice or for direct diagnosis and treatment of a medical condition by a qualified
physician. Readers who have questions about a particular condition, possible treatments
for that condition, or possible reactions from the condition or its treatment should consult
a physician or other qualified healthcare professional.